T0067143

You are hunted by the Jewel wasp

by the

Humans have been controlled throughout history, but there is a way for you to become yourself.

www.YouAreHuntedByTheJewelWasp.com

Simon Proctor

authorHOUSE®

AuthorHouse™ UK
1663 Liberty Drive
Bloomington, IN 47403 USA
www.authorhouse.co.uk
Phone: 0800.197.4150

Published by AuthorHouse 04/17/2015

ISBN: 978-1-4969-9571-1 (sc)
ISBN: 978-1-4969-9824-8 (e)

This book is dedicated to you and your success.

"Absorb what is useful, discard what is not.

Add what is uniquely your own."

Bruce Lee

CONTENTS

ACKNOWLEDGEMENTS

This is a special book for me. It brings together all my personal experiences, studies and research. As a successful person, I have been through the process you will read about and each step has given me something new and taught me many valuable lessons. Writing this book has shown me just how much I've gained from failure and success.

In terms of writing the book, there have been many outstanding people who have encouraged me by their precious lessons such as:

Napoleon Hill, Osho, Richard Dawkins, Abraham Hicks, Wallace D. Wattles, Fred Alan Wolf, Dr Joe Vitale, Ralph Waldo Emerson, Dr Joseph Murphy, Les Brown, Bob Proctor, Robert Kiyosaki, Nik Halik, Molana Jalal-e-Din Mohammad Molavi Rumi, Brian Tracy, Dr Daniel G. Amen, Bruce Lee, James Allen, Jack Canfield, Thomas J. Stanley, Spencer Johnson, Rhonda Byrne, Earl Nightingale, Buddha and Yanni.

My dear mother just always believed in me and supported me in delivering a book that I hope will add real value and help you make the very best of your life.

I greatly appreciate my brothers and sister for their support and unconditional love.

I acknowledge my fiancée, Nabby, for her assistance, patience, guidance, and support for this project. Without her, this book would never have been written.

I also appreciate the many contributions made by all great teachers around the world who have taught me or others even one small lesson.

INTRODUCTION

The hardest situation in your life holds your greatest bliss.
Author's Introduction:
I hate poverty!

I don't respect poverty, I don't appreciate poverty.

It is out of stupidity that people are poor; it is due to the beliefs of superstitious minds that people are poor.

People need not be poor.

It is because for thousands of years we have been taught that poverty has something spiritual in it that people are poor. (By: Osho.)

Today's fly was a dream yesterday and today's dream will come true tomorrow. Believe in yourself to make your dreams come true. (By: Mr Mohammad Morghi.)

Everything began with a small spark in my brain or a mysterious power in my mind and soul. I had a very hard time. My family was so poor. We lived in a half-built house with very poor facilities and I suffered very much. I escaped from military service not because of a fear of war or the hardships of a soldier, I was a professional martial artist and I frequently won first place in countrywide self-defence and free-fighting championship competitions.

I escaped from military service because I did not want to become a toy in the hands of politicians who might move me in any direction that they wanted. I never cheated by saying: "I am a patriot." From the first history of humankind a few groups of people have dominated the larger population, and they will always rule them, body and soul. But I will define homeland in another way. My homeland is the planet Earth and my flag is the blue sky.

I lay down in a forest park on a sunny day in the shade of pine trees, a wanted man without money, without nationality, without permission to work, without a father and without any relative to help me. It was just me. I was alone, and alone in a very difficult situation, a prisoner body and big dreams in my mind. Then I stopped dreaming and looked at the sky through the tree branches. I had to go home. That ruined home with no walls, no windows and a damaged roof. But no, that was not a safe place because I might get caught. I thought about poverty and I was searching for a door to get out from the prison of poverty in my mind. I thought about freedom, wealth, and a fantasy world in my imagination. I wanted to break the chains that bound me, the chain of religion, the chain of patriotism, the chain of superstition, and the strongest one of all; the chain of poverty.

I floated within these thoughts when suddenly I heard a strong voice inside of me, the voice that made me a painter, made me a poet, and in the midst of poverty made me an author and made me a national martial arts champion. That voice had a very strong energy and it will stay with me forever. That voice made me a successful businessman and a professional manager. On that day the voice shouted at me to escape from my country. I had no money. I was a wanted man and I did not know anybody who could help me to escape from my country illegally. And illegal escape was the only option I had, because I had no passport and I couldn't get one, and if I stayed any longer I could be killed in my home, like my father, in front of his children for the reason of integrity. *No*, my inner force shouted, *you have to go. Fly out. GO. Go to a peaceful place and heal your wounds*. I surrendered to this desire. I stood up and said to myself: "I will go."

I went through prison, hunger, danger, betrayal, pain of soul and body and death, and never gave up. Today I have achieved all my ambitions, I have beaten poverty and founded a big commercial company. I work few hours and make a lot of money. I live in peace, bliss and love. I have come a long way and learnt a lot. My purpose in writing this book is not to write my biography. Because my life story includes such weird and complex events, I may never write it, but I have a very big gift for you. I will show you the path to wealth, the path that I discovered based on my own studies and experiences.

You may be born into a working or middle class family, or maybe you are an employee; or maybe you're a rich person. Despite your current social status you should pay attention to a key fact: all of the rich men and women in history have followed certain rules of wealth. These rules are unchangeable and they work for anybody that applies them. Here I must define the meaning of richness once again: a rich person is a person who lives in full peace, and has financial and spiritual power, and brings happiness and bliss to the lives of others. A real rich person is powerful internally and externally. A spiritual person who has a poor physical life, or a person who has lots of money but suffers from inner conflicts, can never be considered to be a wealthy person. A person who balances all inner and outer energies to enhance their personality and rise up is a real wealthy person.

Read this book in peace and neutrality. You will find an unusual force that enables you to do anything you want. The source and performance of this force is as yet unknown to scientists. This force is proven by its magical power. You have this force inside of you all the time and it connects you to the world. All of your dreams are ready inside of you and this book will teach you how to manifest them. I promise you can win if you want to. There are many men and women in history who have created anything they wanted from nothing, things that are hard to imagine, let alone to achieve. You can achieve anything you want just by being in harmony with the rules of universe. I will teach you how to balance your dreams and your world, and finally you can create your own life. I believe wholeheartedly that you can have anything that you want.

Read this book over and over again until you understand it.

CHAPTER 1

Why I wrote this book?

In 2005 a new game show-*Deal Or No Deal*, hosted by Noel Edmonds-burst onto UK television screens and resurrected for him what had become a stagnant career. A year or so after that, Edmonds claimed to have manifested the opportunity to present the show using a system called cosmic ordering. Around about the same time a book (later a film, too) called *The Secret* took the world by storm. It explained the Law of Attraction and asserted that you could use it to your advantage and learn to manifest whatever you wanted.

Despite this, not everyone who tried to use cosmic ordering or the Law of Attraction ended up with what they wanted; some ended up with nothing, others ended up worse off than before they started.

Over the course of my lifetime I have experienced many things and learned a great deal, and I believe I know why some people get what they want and others don't. I have myself created and shaped a fantastic, successful life using universal truths and laws, and that's why I felt I had to write this book; to tell people what I had learned and achieved and to let you know that you can do it, too.

In this book you will read about your own inner power, and also come to understand how you are controlled and prevented from using this power. That is perhaps the biggest obstacle you face when it comes to generating wealth and becoming rich.

We're going to look at people's attitudes to money and to riches, and you will gain some fascinating insights into just what might be holding you back. We'll also look at some stories about successful people to show you that what stops you is in your mind.

You will learn about the universal laws that will allow you to have your heart's desire.

And I will tell you how to put all this new knowledge to work with a step by step guide to becoming wealthy and successful. As a result of reading this book and putting into practice what it teaches you, you will be able to follow your dream, no matter how big that dream may be.

1

You just have to learn and follow the universal laws; tell the universe what you want and wait for it to come to you.

Changing your life is a challenge and an adventure; life is an exciting journey and by reading this book, you're already taking the first steps towards a brighter tomorrow.

CHAPTER 2

Why isn't everyone rich?

"Anybody can wish for riches, and most people do, but only a few know that a definite plan, plus a burning desire for wealth, are the only dependable means of accumulating wealth."

Napoleon Hill

If any one of us can have anything we want, why are we not all billionaires?

That seems to be a reasonable question, don't you think? Well, the answer might not be the one you want to hear; it is very often because we do not believe we could be that wealthy, or even that we should be. It says in the Bible that "the love of money is the root of all evil" (1 Timothy 6:10). Why should we wish for something that is evil?

Let me tell you something, I believe it is the lack of money that is the root of all evil, not the love of it. Poverty is evil. For some reason there are people who think that there is some spiritual benefit in being poor, but there is nothing spiritual about not having a coat that keeps out the cold, shoes that keep out the rain, or seeing your children cry themselves to sleep because there is no money for food.

Everyone needs money. Everyone wants to be rich but, not everyone believes they deserve it.

But know this; a life of abundance and comfort is your birthright. You were not put upon this earth to suffer; you were put here to thrive and to grow and to prosper. You do deserve it and truly believing that you do is an important step towards getting what you want.

If you are someone who always puts the needs of others before your own needs, you must change that mindset. You do not have to become selfish and to stop caring about others, I'm not saying that, but you do have to accept that you are as important as they are. You are worthy. You are valuable. And you deserve to get what you desire, too. It is possible to be humble while also valuing your true self. It is not humble to always put yourself last and to feel you are unworthy; it is foolish and it denies the beauty and magnificence of life; your life.

Believe in yourself; the mind is fertile ground and will grow whatever is planted. Allow your self-belief to flourish and flower and you will reap the benefits.

CHAPTER 3

Attitudes of people toward wealth

"Be like water making its way through cracks. Do not be assertive, but adjust to the object, and you shall find a way around or through it. If nothing within you stays rigid, outward things will disclose themselves. Empty your mind, be formless. Shapeless, like water. If you put water into a cup, it becomes the cup. You put water into a bottle and it becomes the bottle. You put it in a teapot, it becomes the teapot. Now, water can flow or it can crash. Be water, my friend."

Bruce Lee

I mentioned in the last chapter that there are some people who believe poverty is good for the soul. That is just one attitude towards wealth. I gave the matter a great deal of thought and I divided the various attitudes of people toward wealth into five categories:
1. People who do not want wealth because they believe it will lead them away from God and humanity.
2. People who want wealth, but don't know how to achieve it.
3. People who want wealth and know some ways of achieving it, but are unable to get ahead.
4. People who are wealthy, but have a suffering life.
5. People who want wealth and are wealthy and apply the right rules towards getting wealthy.

1. People who do not want wealth because they believe it will lead them away from God and humanity

I am sure that you are not in group 1. Because people who believe wealth is an evil thing would never buy a book like this and never identify with such a person. They believe these things are evil. They imprison themselves inside of poverty, misery and a vacuum. They are patsies under full control. They believe that if they avoid life's blessings, they will achieve total spirituality and ultimate kingship.

But many of them have escaped from these nonsense thoughts and they are not in group one anymore. You should know a good teacher who teaches true humanity, never teaches poverty.

2. People who want wealth, but don't know how to achieve it

There are people who want to be wealthy, but they don't know how to achieve it and they believe it is impossible. These people suffer from a lack of self-efficacy and are intensely influenced by environment. They can't find a way to wealth because they believe it is impossible, so they do not search. Usually they think like this:

I was born in a poor family.
I have no support.
I haven't needed an education.
I haven't friends and relatives.
I haven't any money to start with.
I am spiritually very weak.
It is very late for me to start.
The economy has collapsed.
I stand no chance in the environment that I live in.
My wife/husband is a barrier to my success.
The government is a barrier to my success.
I am not lucky.

And many more, that not only create financial poverty for them, but also make them ill, physically and mentally. They missed this simple rule; that we will live according to our beliefs.

The goal of this book is to help people to believe in themselves. It is possible to start from nothing and achieve everything. You can be one of the future's billionaires. This is a truth. There are some fixed rules related to becoming rich that anyone can apply.

Nothing happens by chance. Chance is another word for lack of knowledge about something. But do not fool yourself. Every self-made millionaire has followed the same rules. And you can be the next one. Everything starts from the mind and the way of thinking. Thoughts are nothing physically, but you can start something from that powerful nothing. Everything starts from nothing; that is a principle.

3. People who want wealth and know some ways of achieving it but, are unable to get ahead

People who want to be rich but who remain in the working or middle classes believe as a result of research and study that if they are in harmony and follow specific rules, they will achieve wealth. The logical and experimental part of their brain easily accepts that there are definite ways to get rich and nothing happens by chance. But despite this they stay poor or become only moderately wealthy.

Let me cite an example. One day I read the Highway Code and I passed the theory exam. I memorized everything and I accepted that if I learned the rules of driving I would be safe from accident and injury. In other words my logical mind accepted that any driver has to learn these rules and follow them. But when I sat behind the wheel for the first time and started to drive on the road, I didn't follow most of the rules that I learnt and believed to be right.

Sometimes I didn't turn on the indicator, didn't check the mirrors, put the car into the wrong gear, ignored a red light, didn't follow road priorities, didn't pay attention to pedestrians and made many more mistakes, any one of which was enough to put someone's life in danger. But I am in the process of learning and my instructor sits beside me and alerts me to danger or takes control of the car when necessary.

But why was I still making mistakes, despite having passed the theory exam? Why couldn't I drive appropriately, despite knowing everything about driving correctly? Just like those people who wanted to be rich (I wanted to be able to drive, too) they know the rules of how to get rich and they would get an "A" if there was an exam in how to get rich (just like me in driving), but they are still poor or only moderately wealthy because they do not apply their knowledge. (Just like me when I made dangerous mistakes when driving.)

The mind consists of two parts, conscious and unconscious (that are discussed separately). We influence the conscious part through studying, researching, analysing, intuition and other guidance, and record the results for specific reasons. But these results cannot change our behaviour and actions until they are recorded into our unconscious mind, when they turn into deep beliefs. Unconsciousness records any data that we gather from the environment with our five senses and then moves us based on a pre-determined plan, although usually we are not aware of these plans.

If we snap back to my driving example, my unconsciousness was not coded appropriately to make me a skilful driver. After I put into action the lessons that I learnt and I practise, practise and practise, and I repeat and repeat and repeat, I can instil good driving skills into my unconsciousness. This is the only way to create a good driver. It is also true with regard to getting rich.

You need:

- Awareness of the truth that your mind has been controlled by others for a long time.
- A burning desire to achieve wealth.
- To have faith and believe that it is possible to get rich in any situation.
- Knowledge about the ways of getting rich (and the rules of it, such as paying attention to body, soul, love, target, emotional control and independence).
- Discipline.
- Patience.
- Implementation.
- Appropriate use of wealth.

4. People who are wealthy, but have a suffering life

People who want to be rich and are already rich, but have a painful life. I remember my brother when he wanted to own a motorcycle. He was working hard to achieve his desire. Finally he purchased a beautiful motorcycle, but one day he had a terrible accident that broke his arm and head and he lost one of his legs. Doctors transplanted another leg, but due to extreme infection they had to remove it. Today he lives with an artificial leg. He still has a motorcycle, but his life is so painful. He always thinks about the motorcycle but he never tries to learn how to use it. He also never tries to understand himself and his own abilities. He was driving drunk, he was often drunk, anxious, and angry, and he was blaming others for his own failures.

Similarly there are some rich people who have a painful life for two reasons. First, they do not know the appropriate use of wealth and second, they do not work on themselves to achieve self-efficacy. True wealth is being rich internally and externally. Physical wealth or money is a type of energy. Yes, money is a kind of energy like every other thing in the world. It is neither good nor bad, not positive and not negative. We give meaning to money by how we use it. Money helps a bad person to become worse and harm himself and others. And money also helps a good person to be a better servant for him and for the world. I do not want to speak about the philosophy of bad and good, but I want to explain briefly how I define them for myself.

I think goodness is peace, the love of yourself and others serves the world with sympathy and a sense of unity with the entire world, gratitude and any other feeling that creates a good mood and a healthful inner world in a person and his environment. I call any feeling that hurts us or others a bad one. So we conclude we have to try to achieve wealth AND we also have to learn how to use it appropriately. Many people say: "I will learn it when I get rich," just like my brother, who said, "I will learn how to drive it when I buy it." But it's wrong. You must know how to use your wealth right now.

5. People who want wealth and are wealthy and apply the right rules towards getting wealthy

The person who follows all the laws in this book will be known by all as a wealthy and wise person.

CHAPTER 4

You are under control

"It wouldn't be mind control, if you will know you've been under mind control."

VicDo

Listen to me; pay close attention to what you read in this chapter. Read it word by word in a loud voice and at the same time that you read this, with eyes wide and your entire mind open, look around you and see how ruthlessly people are being killed in the name of earth, nationality, flag, ethic, faction, religion and God. People are very much like the sheep that are in the control of their shepherd. Don't be stupid; have a good look around you. Think, because you too are one of those under control and if you understand more than most people, the powers that be will offer you money, position and power to keep you quiet. They might offer you the chance to control a small part of their dirty game. If you don't accept the money and their power they might even take your life. They even wrote the Human Rights laws to control you. If you look closely you will see that human rights do not apply in the world. The reason that they have created this concept of human rights is exactly the same reason they created God. These are their tools to control you more easily. Through every belief and credence that they plant in your mind, they will take advantage of you. They can even control your natural bodily abilities, such as sex.

I have no interest in politics or the Gods that they have created. I am not part of any association, party or minority. I am free and I have a desire to teach you how you too could become free. Before taking any other step you need to break all the controlling chains around you.

There are lots of books which are easy to read, understand and apply, books which teach you that you will achieve all your desires simply by thinking and imagining them in your mind; as they say, you are what you think about.

You can achieve whatever goal you have in life by just thinking fundamentally about what you want. Books and mentors that teach you how the Law of Attraction works, will tell you about all the universal laws. These laws are effective and correct, but there is a missing part. In fact, a huge part is missing. Many of those who have a burning desire for success attend seminars and conferences, and buy books and DVDs. They study books which teach them how they can become successful. They attend online or actual classes that teach them what they need to do to become a successful person. Some will pay a successful person to be their personal mentor. All of these actions are necessary, but they are just one part of the path you must follow to become free, happy and successful.

Nevertheless, have you ever thought why these books, DVDs, mentors and so on don't work for everyone? Why in many cases people just lose their valuable time and money?

Do you know that even some of these people who have achieved their desires – such as buying a huge house, getting lots of money into their bank accounts, finding a great career, having a perfect partner in life and many more – don't yet feel prosperous? If they felt successful, it only lasted for a short time.

Have you ever thought why some people run their entire life to find success? Because they have been running in something very similar to a rat race and only when they are about to pass away from this universe do they realize that have not achieved their desires.

I will give you the answers to all these questions and will teach you the ultimate way of achieving lasting success. However, at the end of the day it's you who must decide to go along this path and let me tell you this now, it won't be easy.

As I mentioned before there are many great books about the laws of the universe and secrets of success, as well as some knowledgeable mentors who teach these laws and secrets, and to go down this path you will need them.

However, most of these teachers and mentors don't teach you the first step, which it is essential to know. You need to find a mentor who is aware of brain function, someone like Bob Proctor who can teach you about the conscious and unconscious mind. Mentors who begin from the first and the most important step will show you that you are under control and also that you act like a programmed robot.

Once you understand that, they can teach you how to break all those chains of control and you – and only you – will then decide what you want for your own life. The reason for this is that before you decide what you want in your life, you need to make sure it is what you desire without any influence from the outside world. A pure and burning desire can only manifest when you are aware of the controlling power in the world and know that there is not any universal influence on you. The reason that I am not labeling the universal laws with a positive or negative is that it is up to you to decide.

In this book you will come across references to controlling power a lot. For instance, leaders of countries, governments and religious leaders control people, and from the very first moment of birth they begin programming people's minds.

You should know that we cannot really see the principals, and that all the kings, queens, prime ministers, presidents, religious leaders, etc., are themselves puppets under the principals' hands and, just like viruses and parasitism, the principals hide themselves because in order to continue living they should not show their face.

When I say they are hiding I don't mean that they are hiding in a house or a city. They move among us. They will never talk about their true identity and you may never know that he had taken many years of your precious life just by controlling you from outside. They have an incredible recondite system and organization that won't be found easily.

The truth is that you don't need to know them or see them; you just ought to know that you are being controlled by them.

These people also think they are more intelligent than you, and they can do a better job by thinking for you and can lead you better than you could yourself.

They imagine they are rendering a service to you; however, what they do can destroy you. Even some parents have the bad habit of making decisions for their child when he needs to learn how to take responsibility and make their own decisions. Of course parents should make decisions for their children when they are very young, but then again children need to learn about responsibility and make decisions with the supervision of their parents.

Countries throughout the world have to be controlled by important rules and laws; it is a fact that some are essential. For example, it is necessary to have specified laws for driving in the street, or to import and export goods, etc.

To maintain safety we have to have some rules. All of these laws and rules are essential for every society. These are just a few examples to show you that when I say we have to break the control chain I don't mean we should break these laws. Furthermore, in some situations you should give your control to someone else because that would be the best option. For example, when you are sick and see a doctor, you will follow his guidance to get better, because he has specialist knowledge.

You should be capable of distinguishing between an essential law – which is for your benefit - and a law that will destroy your life.

I neither aim to nix, despise nor scorn your mentality with regard to country leaders, religious leaders, governments or God. No, no, I don't judge them at all, because that's their nature. Governments and religions mean controlling people and cannot be anything else. History provides great evidence to confirm that these controlling powers from governments and religion will always be there, just like the story of the frog and the scorpion.

In the story, a scorpion and a frog are good friends. They meet on the bank of a stream and the scorpion asks the frog to carry him across on its back. The frog asks, "How do I know you won't sting me?" The scorpion says, "Because if I do, I will die too." The frog is satisfied, and they set out, but in midstream, the scorpion stings the frog. The frog feels the onset of paralysis and starts to sink, knowing they both will drown, but has just enough time to gasp "Why?" The scorpion replies: "I am sorry, it's my nature..."

Scorpions are those who control your mind and you are the frog that has created a logical philosophy for itself and says that scorpion won't sting me because otherwise he will die, too. Many of you will do the same thing and will trust the scorpion and this story is repeating every day. I don't want to judge either scorpion or the frog and if there needs to be a judgement, it should be for the creator of these creatures.

There is only one difference between the frog and humans in this story and that is humans have the ability to understand things, be aware and do not be in control.

When you understand this instead of dying by the sting of the scorpion you can make a medicine from its poison.

When you learn that you are not living for yourself, when you realize that you are an eagle among prairie chickens, and you have been programmed to eat only grubs and worms and live like a prairie chicken and die as a prairie chicken.

When you understand and decide to be yourself and only you make decisions for your life, when you have erased all the beliefs and credence that was seeded in your unconscious mind. When you learn that you should not fear anything. When you become aware that you ought not to label your actions as sinful or good. When you learn that you should accept yourself completely and have learned to love yourself, then it's time to begin. You are like a building that was built by a million people, but now you have the power to demolish that structure and build in its place a phenomenal building, just as you'd like it to be.

This is a very tough job, it's exhausting and onerous.

To break yourself and build it again, you must pay a huge cost.

You need to have burning desire, be patient, be consistent; you should not give up in any case; you should have faith in yourself, and you can learn from incredible teachers such as Les Brown, Bob Proctor, Esther Hicks, Napoleon Hill and many more.

Always remember that your greatest and ultimate guide is you, yourself.

You can discipline yourself when you learn to look at life more deeply.

CHAPTER 5

How they control you?

"To find out who rules over you, simply find out who you are not allowed to criticize."

Voltaire

Ask yourself, am I being true to myself? Am I moving in a direction that I want to move in? And are my choices affected by external factors?

If you pay attention to yourself you will find you are like a programmed computer and this means you are affected by external factors. The clothes that you wear, foods that you eat, your religion, your political viewpoint, your language-even your accent-and, above all, your thoughts... if you focus on these aspects of your life you will come to a terrible conclusion: you are controlled.

Nikola Tesla said: "The human being is a self-propelled automaton entirely under the control of external influences. Willful and predetermined though they appear, his actions are governed not from within, but from without. He is like a float tossed about by the waves of a turbulent sea."

In a street full of criminals most of newborn babies will grow up to be criminals and it is also true for babies born in poor streets that they will grow up to be poor. Why does a Muslim country remain Muslim? Or a Christian country remains Christian? You can ask yourself many more questions. How can a few people dominate a large population? Remember this excellent quotation from Napoleon: "Imagination rules the world." You may not agree with him, you may say: "Wealth rules the world." But if you think profoundly you will find the roots of wealth inside of thoughts, and also the roots of any other entity. James Allen defines the power of thoughts absolutely and reveals this secret: that everything starts with thoughts. He says:

"Only by much searching and mining are gold and diamonds obtained, and man can find every truth connected with his being if he will dig deep into the mine of his soul. And that he is the maker of his character, the molder of his life, and the builder of his destiny, he may unerringly prove: if he will watch, control, and alter his thoughts, tracing their effects upon himself, upon others, and upon his life and circumstances; if he will link cause and effect by patient practice and investigation, utilizing his every experience, even to the most trivial, as a means of obtaining that knowledge of himself. In this direction, as in no other, is the law absolute that 'He that seeketh findeth; and to him that knocketh it shall be opened,' for only by patience, practice, and ceaseless importunity can a man enter the Door of the Temple of Knowledge." (From chapter one of *As a Man Thinketh*, by James Allen.)

Napoleon Hill studied more than five hundred men and women and concluded that everything starts just by thoughts. He states in his wonderful book, *Think and Grow Rich*, that "all achievements and all earned riches have their beginning in an IDEA."

These enlightened people teach you the greatest secret of happiness and bliss (or misery) and this secret hides just in your mind. You should believe anything starts just by a thought in your mind. But also you should clarify whether these thoughts are your true thoughts and do they come from your heart, or are they dictated to you by the environment that you live in?

You come a long way when you become aware that you are controlled by external factors. From this point you will never allow anyone to affect your thoughts from outside again. And you turn a page with your thoughts and code a new programme in your unconscious mind.

Here I remember the terrific lectures of George Carlin. He spoke about true owners, great owners, and rich men who control big decisions. He told us: Do not take politicians too seriously. Your thoughts are not related to them. They are employed to induce you to think you have freedom to choose, but you don't. You have not any choice, you have an owner. They are your owners and they own everything, they own all important lands and they control companies. They bought parliament, legislature, congress and municipals long ago. They control judges and they own all the news media. They control all the news you hear every day. You are within their hands and they spend millions of dollars to advertise anything they want. We know what they want; they want to put our thoughts in complete control. But let me say what they don't want. They don't want a society full of sophisticated critics. They don't want smart people who realize how they were thrown overboard thirty years ago and eliminated by such a system. They don't want this. Do you know what they want? They want just a group of obedient workers, people who have a little intelligence, just enough for moving society's wheels and doing paperwork, and the people are stupid as they do more and more work without any complaint. They want people who work a lot of hours for little wages and lower profit and are overloaded with work. And do you know they will get back all of the money that they paid you very soon because they are the fucking owners of this country. This is a huge club that you are not registered with. (George Carlin, 1937-2008.)

What it means is that the government wants people to follow their rules. If we imagine a country to be a car, then I believe that the people are the wheels and the body is the government. They give guidance and believe that society should just follow. By governments I don't mean government's employees, because they are just puppets, and behind them there are leaders who give orders.

George Carlin figured out this secret and he tried to tell us we are under control unknowingly. A few people know this secret and a few of them could escape from this trap and create their own thoughts and their own life.

In the next chapter we explain some of most powerful ways that the environment uses to control our minds.

CHAPTER 6

Control by the five senses

"Some of us learn control, more or less by accident. The rest of us go all our lives not even understanding how it is possible, and blaming our failure on being born the wrong way."

B.F. Skinner

A human being can be controlled by his five senses. This method is used by media such as TV, cinema, music, radio, newspapers, magazines, books, computer and Internet games. In this case, they influence the unconscious mind of a person and control him just by eyes and ears. You are a controller or else you are controlled. They affect the nervous system of the brain and make a person happy, sad, angry or horny to perform based on predetermined goals and programmes that are injected into brain. Let me cite some examples: do you watch TV commercials? All the pictures and characters that are shown in these have messages for you that affect you unintentionally. In body building powders commercials there are always some beautiful girls beside the handsome and masculine men. The message is so simple: if you use this powder you will attract beautiful and sexy girls or handsome men. It is also true that at auto exhibitions they use beautiful girls with sexy clothes not as sales specialists, but to attract people.

Many people suffer from weight problems. Recently there are more fat people shown in commercials than there were before. Do you know what the reason is? Because overweight people who see those commercials feel better about themselves and say: "OK, so being overweight is not as terrible as I thought."

As you see, TV programmes are a very practical tool for governments to use to inject their opinions and desires into the mind of society. Actually you have no influence over this because they make the decisions about programmes and about commercials and their messages. You may ask, "How can I avoid this?" The answer is so simple. There is an "off" button on every television!

Family, friends and relatives may also affect your senses, and control you unintentionally. For example, imagine a teenager who comes home.

Teenager: he enters the room and shouts, "Hey, Mum, I've decided to travel around the world to see new people, new cultures and new countries. I want to discover the world."

Mum: "Don't say that, son, it is not rational. Do you know it takes lots of money? And do you know we live in a world that is full of war and violence? What happens if they take you hostage? What happens if they kill you for your skin colour or hurt you for your money, or kill you in a street war? Don't you see the news? Come here and watch TV and see how many terrible things happen in the world, or take the newspaper from your dad and read the news. Don't you read your school books? History, social sciences and…"

What a pity for the young boy. He learns that the world is full of difficulties and he just has to work, obey, pay taxes, and live in a small rented house; even if he buys his home, he has to pay the bank. If he doesn't pursue an education, he may relate his failures to his lack of education and say: "I wish I'd listened to my parents' advice and pursued my education." He forgets the fact that lots of educated people are controlled by non-educated people.

CHAPTER 7

Sex

"Sex desire is the most powerful of human desires. When driven by this desire, men develop keenness of imagination, courage, will-power, persistence, and creative ability unknown to them at other times."

Napoleon Hill

When you understand what the government has done with you, you will be shocked.

From the first second that you were born you have been programmed and made into a human robot without your permission.

They know how your mind and soul work and are very professional in that.

Sex is another super power in human beings; by getting to know it and controlling it, it will allow you to get what you desire.

They don't let you use this super power correctly and efficiently. They don't want you to understand and comprehend sex. The reason for this is because then they can't control you.

Let me tell about one of the million examples that exist in history.

Hundreds year ago there was a person called Hassan Sabbah who was claiming that he was a prophet from God.

He was commanded to gather together some of the most desperate soldiers for his special missions. He called them Fedayeen, which means they were happy to die for the success of the mission.

One of the important things that could help a soldier to become a Fedayeen was to be celibate. Sabbah wasn't just depriving them of having a baby, "celibacy" was meant to divest a man from enjoying sex altogether, and the reason for this was because Sabbah was a wise man and he knew all about sexual power. He knew that if he allowed them to use their sexual power he couldn't control them in the way he wanted to and they might refuse to follow his commandments. He believed that sexual power was greater than the power of any governor.

History is full of this type of story and there are now and will be forever people controlled in this way.

All governors and religious leaders are aware of this phenomenal power and today they are trying to control their societies with it by labeling it sin, crime, mistake, illness, etc.

They do this to keep you only on the path that they want you to be on. They want couples to live with the fear of wrongdoing and to worry about what if he/she cheats on me, what if I am disobeying God by having sex and what if having sex before marriage is wrong? You have been frightened of this precious power. While you have dread in your unconscious mind you can't pass the barriers and know sex. You only think of it and fight against it if you too had been influenced.

All of these can cause sexual deviation, depression, anxiety, and feelings of guilt, and these can easily destroy your life.

The truth is that if you want to enjoy your life in its full meaning, and achieve great success and wealth in your life, you must let go of these thoughts.

The only way to be free is to stop following the hand-made rules of religious leaders. It is they who let the seed of fear and guilt grow in you.

Enjoy sex, don't feel guilty about doing it, but always use the latest hygiene principles to avoid illness.

Sex is beautiful, sex is a type of meditation, sex will give you calmness and wellness, sex can keep you young and happy, sex can improve your imagination and can make you closer to you! And you know what? One will experience the ultimate prosperity, wealth and wisdom only when one feels true sex.

You might be married. I am sure if you are surrounded by religion, religious leaders and your society, you won't be able to enjoy sex like you did in the first few years of your marriage. You cannot have an orgasm if you adjudge yourself to have the same sexual relationship forever. You are under so much influence that if in private and in your mind you ever think of having sex with someone else, you feel guilty and you feel you are being disloyal. You might fear what others would say or think of you, you might be afraid of doing it because people call it sin or you might be eschewing from hell and continue to live like a piece of soulless meat.

21

You may fear finding out that your partner has had an affair with someone, and you would feel that he/she was a traitor to you if they did, because you have been taught that by others around you. You know that you might have thought of this situation a number of times.

The truth is that in most cases people in that situation would think that their partner doesn't love them anymore and they have to get divorced or separated and some people would feel their partner has humiliated them.

Love is so much greater and more powerful than a sexual relationship and you must know that sex with all its power cannot stand in front of a true love.

If your partner had sex with someone else and began feeling for him then that's a good sign; it shows that he didn't really love you, because sex neither can compete with love nor be the reason for loving someone.

So if you ever face such a situation be happy and grateful because there wasn't a true love from your partner and if this affair hadn't happened you could never have seen the true side of your partner and you might have an unpleasant life together. You should not become overly depressed by this situation and you can be sure that your life will become happier and more pleasant than before and you can focus on your desires in life and finally you will experience true success and happiness.

Know that if you prevent sexual power manifesting in your life, it will always appear in a negative way. However, if you get to know your sexual power and begin using it you will be amazed by its strength and will be prosperous and successful in every single way that you can think of.

CHAPTER 8

Inner sense, best guidance

"Every time you don't follow your inner guidance, you feel a loss of energy, loss of power, a sense of spiritual deadness."

Shakti Gawin

We can easily identify any thoughts, actions, situations or people that make us feel bad. This is so simple.

You just need to be aware of your emotions, because this is the best way to identify the cause of a negative mood such as jealousy, revenge, hatred, humility, fear, disappointment, helplessness, poverty etc., and these negative feelings both have a harmful effect on your brain performance and interrupt the process of right thinking.

If you stay in a negative mood for a long time, you will become depressed or stressed. Scientists indicate that long-term stress is among the causes of heart disease, senescence of cellules and various other diseases.

Some research indicates that bad experiences early in life could be a cause of long-term illness. But this is not true just for childhood experiences; it includes any mental tension such as anxiety and negative excitation that interrupts an organ's mechanism. Stress is a starting point for physical diseases, especially heart disease. As noted before, you can identify anything that makes you feel bad. You may tell me, "I knew all of these things." You may know you are controlled by external factors or perhaps you knew negative thoughts make you feel bad.

I'm sure you are aware of the side effects of negative emotion on your body and life. I was, too, even before I started my research into becoming rich and successful. I was aware of my bad feelings and I knew which situations made me stressful and worried, and why. I knew that diseases and death are most common in poor people rather than rich, successful ones. I was not a scientist, but I was aware of the harmful influences of negative emotions on my body and my life. (Just like you, who knows many things.)

Although we are brainwashed with false beliefs in school, the family, society and religious places, they teach us some good things, too. They teach us which thoughts are harmful and which actions or people make us scared or worried, which TV channels should never be watched and which places should be avoided. They teach us what foods are good for our body and what are bad.

They teach us many good things, so why are there so many people trapped in poverty and dogged by worry, sadness and disease? There is a problem, definitely. It is impossible that someone should know everything about wealth and happiness and yet die in misery. There is a thing that we need to know in order to be in control, but that we never learn. Here is a secret, a secret that they don't teach us, a secret that we all know, see, hear and feel, but never profoundly perceive. We seek to find the key of paradise just when we have a burning desire to achieve success and wealth and just when we believe in our ultimate power. And at this point we are faced with masters, books and people who help us to learn and guide us to a path that I call "Paradise Road". In this book you will learn the thing that they don't teach you.

Gradually you start to perceive the secret of universal creation and you will figure out that you are the creator of your life. Those people who control our minds do not want us to know we are a Godlike creature. In all the good things that they teach us there is a drop of poison. And just like a glass of water that you drop poison into, even one drop is enough to kill us. They never tell us we could have our water pure from a fountain and they never tell us there is a drop of poison in our glass of water. Yes, of course they teach us good things, but just one drop of poison is enough to spoil everything.

They control our brain system to move us in any direction that they want. This action is very similar to the way a particular type of wasp operates. It's a good example to show how societies are controlled by a number of small groups.

The Jewel wasp – also known as the emerald cockroach wasp – is actually able to control the mind of a cockroach. Without this ability the cockroach, which is up to six times larger than the wasp, would definitely have the upper hand; once injected with venom, however, the cockroach is under the control of the wasp.

Gaining control is a two-stage process. First venom is injected into the midsection of the cockroach, temporarily paralysing it. Once the cockroach has been disabled, a second shot of venom is injected with surgical precision into precisely the section of the brain which controls the flight reflex. Bizarrely, the cockroach spends the next half hour or so obsessively grooming, giving the wasp time to go and find a burrow and prepare it for the cockroach.

When she returns, the wasp bites off around half of each of the cockroach's antennae, feeding on the fluids released to replenish her strength after her exertions; the poor zombified cockroach doesn't even try to fight back. Being smaller in size, the only way the wasp can get the cockroach to its burrow is to get it to walk there, and it does this by biting on one of the half-eaten antennae, leading it along then guiding it inside. The cockroach, meek as a lamb, does the wasp's bidding.

Once inside, the wasp lays an egg on the cockroach, then exits the burrow and seals up the entrance. After a few days the egg hatches, and the larva uses the docile cockroach as food, first chewing its way into the abdomen, then eating the internal organs, and finally creating a cocoon inside the cockroach from which it hatches several weeks later.

Jewel wasps are distinctive in appearance, with a metallic blue-green body and red legs, and are normally found in the tropical regions of Africa, South Asia and the Pacific islands. Jewel wasps mate only once, after which the female is able to produce several dozen fertilized eggs – leading to potentially several dozen zombified cockroaches.

While there are other parasites which control the behaviour of their hosts, the Jewel wasp is the only one known to inject venom directly into its host's brain. It works by controlling the release of a neurotransmitter called octapamine, which performs a similar function to noradrenaline in humans. With that function disabled, scarily it's not that the cockroach can't run away, it's that it chooses not to.

The Jewel wasp is one-of-a-kind, but there are other parasites that control their prey's behaviour in several ways. Makes you wonder at how amazing-yet-scary nature is.

When I described the story of the Jewel wasp and its similarity to group controlling performance to one of my well-known friends; he did not agree with me and he replied:

"We always blame external conditions for our failures, just like the example that you mentioned about the wasp. You are wrong and you want to throw the blame on to environment and situation. Let me explain it more clearly.

"It is true that our external environment is manipulated by some persons or groups for their own benefit. But are they to blame for our

25

failures? Definitely not. How could it be possible? The story is just like this: the environment tries to control our minds. But the mind is ours and we have full authority over it. We can open it up or shut it down to any external influence, just like we choose TV channels to watch, books to read, music and conversation to hear and finally thoughts to think. I do not want you to blame others for your failures, but to be aware that you are the creator of your life and there is a big amount of energy inside of you. You should guard it and keep it safe from external attacks. If you do it you will never be controlled by others."

My friend speaks very nicely and his critique is eloquent. But the story is not as simple as he said. He missed important notes. He forgot that a little child is just like a computer, with free memory that records any details from the environment, a free memory with no decision-making power. That little child has not the authority to ignore TV programmes or a family member's negative impression of him and then go and choose a better family. Is it possible that a child born in America, who can only understand English, will address her mother in Spanish (*madere*) or her father in French (*père*) or when he becomes hungry say, "*Je suis affamé?*" No, it's impossible. The child speaks only in the language of his parents. Language, religion, culture, what is believed to be ugly, what is believed to be pretty and thousands of other ethical codes, such as our way of thinking, have been recorded unconsciously from our environment without our intervention. The controlling group uses many methods to control minds, and one of them is conditioning.

Perhaps it is not favourable for a positive-thinking and proud person just like my friend. He may state that every child can learn any language after he grows up. But it is rare for someone to speak a foreign language just like the native speakers of that language. Also, it needs lots of effort and practise to learn a new language. But our discussion is more expansive than a specific language or culture. We learn how to think, how to be controlled by others and how to get rich in schools and universities. But they never teach us the exact meaning of money or the ways of positive thinking. Is it possible to turn a destroyed building into a new, strong and neat one immediately? No, it is not an easy task. It needs time, appropriate design, a strong foundation, good materials, professional architects, skilful workers and lots of effort.

There is a big truth about human beings and it is this: if we decide, we have the power to escape from the controlling umbrella of government, religious leaders and others, and be in control of our own lives.

CHAPTER 9

Inner big energy

"All the breaks you need in life wait within your imagination. Imagination is the workshop of your mind, capable of turning mind energy into accomplishment and wealth."

Napoleon Hill

This inner energy will give to you anything you want, anything you desire, but you have to summon it using your mind. This energy is awakened by your thoughts and by your imagination. Anything that you think, visualize and believe will be granted to you by this energy. Nothing is impossible for your inner energy. Great men in history have used this energy to achieve great accomplishments. They flew to the sky, went to other planets, destroyed mountains, traversed oceans, dived into the deeps of the oceans, built palaces and lit them up and manufactured giant machines, discovered the power of electricity, the telephone, the Internet, invented automobiles and trains and much more. All of these things were achieved by persistence in thought and imagination and were created by inner big energy, and it will be the same forever.

Consider what wise men have told us:

"We may divide thinkers into those who think for themselves and those who think through others. The latter are the rule and the former the exception. The first are original thinkers in a double sense and egotists in the noblest meaning of the word."

– Schopenhauer

"The key to every man is his thought. Sturdy and defiant though he look, he has a helm which he obeys, which is the idea after which all his facts are classified. He can only be reformed by showing him a new idea which commands his own."

– Ralph Waldo Emerson

"All truly wise thoughts have been thought already thousands of times; but to make them really ours we must think them over again honestly till they take root in our personal expression."

– Goethe

"All that a man is outwardly is but the expression and completion of his inward thought. To work effectively he must think clearly. To act nobly he must think nobly."

– Channing

"Great men are they who see that spirituality is stronger than any material force; that thoughts rule the world."

– Ralph Waldo Emerson

"Some people study all their lives, and at their death they have learned everything except to think."

– Domergue

"It is the habitual thought that frames itself into our life. It affects us even more than our intimate social relations do. Our confidential friends have not so much to do in shaping our lives as the thoughts have which we harbor."

– J. W. Teal

"When God lets loose a great thinker on this planet, then all things are at risk.

"There is not a piece of science but its flank may be turned tomorrow; or any literary reputation or the so-called eternal names of fame that may not be refused and condemned."

– Ralph Waldo Emerson

THINK! THINK!! THINK!!!

CHAPTER 10

The power of human beings

"A human being is always a child, his power is the power of growth."
Rabindranath Tagore

Many years ago I was a sentimental person. I was writing poems, I was painting; I was searching for something that I lacked. I was suffering from scattered thoughts due to my negative surroundings. I was pouring out my thoughts in poems and paintings, but I was not at peace. And this was not a useful way to achieve peace, because even my poems and paintings were affected by a force outside of me. The difficult aspect of my story was that I couldn't see my target and I didn't know it; but I could feel it. I decided to become a martial artist, a person who has a strong physical power, and a person who is respected by others as a champion. I chose one type of martial arts. I tried a lot and performed very hard physical exercises in very difficult situations and finally I felt it was time to show off my abilities.

I beat all of my peers and kept going forward from urban tournaments to state tournaments and national tournaments. Nobody could defeat me. All of my peers, I knocked out or knocked down. I remember I fought with five competitors on just one day, which was unusual. I knocked out one and knocked down the four others. I was king of the ring, but I was badly injured. My shins were swollen, one of my fingers was broken, and my tendon was stretched, but I felt no pain. I was full of pride and power. I was a professional fighter.

When I returned to my city people were waiting to welcome me. There was my name in the streets, newspapers, magazines and everywhere. After winning first place in a countrywide tournament for two years running, I was chosen to be a trainer of martial arts to the military and teach self-defence to soldiers. But I was unhappy and I didn't like it because I was forced to do that; it was not my goal. I wanted different things, bigger and greater things. There was a voice inside of me that shouted, *be careful; do not allow yourself to be controlled by outside forces.* Finally, after eleven months, I decided to escape from military service and after fighting with one of the commanders I escaped. I was in a good situation there and if I'd obeyed my commanders I could have reached high political and military positions. But I wanted to be controlled just by myself. Now I was a wanted person, without money, permission to work, nationality or support. I eliminated all of my fame and power. My little savings were blocked by the bank and there was nobody to help me.

The voice that advised me to escape from my country did not tell me how I could do so in that situation. But this desire consumed me. I lived in a wooden cottage in a marsh for a long time until my poor mother provided me with a little money so that I could escape from the country illegally. I reached the border and I walked and walked for days and nights. Nothing could stop me. After walking a long way I reached my destination, a country that supported human rights, and I applied for asylum. But a judge found me guilty of entering the country illegally and I was imprisoned. It was a terrible situation, I was in a strange country with a strange culture and language, inside prison and in the company of murderers, addicts and criminals... I wrote down my thoughts and pains on a piece of paper to heal my heart. I wrote one night:

"It's 8 p.m. but the sky is sunny. You damn the sun for making your day longer and my moments deadly. Once again I heard a gentle voice of peace amidst this black, devilish, fearful hell and I am confused by these voices. In this damn hell a breeze is enough to take your life. I look in the mirror and absolutely see the grief in my sunken eyes. But I believe there is a power and there is a light behind these weaknesses that I am faithful to.

"I will get out from this hellfire and then live in a beautiful garden with rivers and birds and sounds of love. I will read again this memo after some months and at that time I will be in a place of ultimate peace and spiritual power. Can I perceive the pain of this moment at that time?

"What bad days and nights I have now; like iron heated inside a furnace and struck by a hammer to create a new shape, I must tolerate this situation. You have to surrender to the strikes or else you will break down. You have to surrender to strikes, not to negative thoughts. It needs time to be reborn and every new birth is indeed painful.

"A new birth is painful for the mother and of course a rebirth of your soul is painful for you, and after these painful moments you will have a new, enlightened life. I will reach the ultimate truth."

I got out of prison after several months. I was in a strange country with no money, no permission to work, no visa, and also no friend, and I didn't know the language. There were many nights I went to sleep hungry because I had no money to buy a piece of bread. The money the government gave to homeless people was so little and it was not enough to live on. I was just thinking, days and nights. I knew there'd been a mistake, definitely, but what was it? Was it from my parents, government or my destiny? I was calling God by various names. I was crying and begging. I took any religion, but couldn't find him. He was not there or if he was, he was completely quiet. I took to complaining, after begging. I screamed: "Damn, where are you?" And then I tore up the Holy Bible. I wished he would burn me for that sin and relieve me from pain because I would prefer to be burned than to suffer. Many years ago some people said to me: "God tests you and if you do not lose your faith in hardship he will finally take your hand and stay with you forever."

One day I asked a pastor why God tests us with pain and difficulties. He replied: "God never does that. Evil does it." I asked again: "Why does God not prevent evil from doing that?" He replied: "Human beings are free to choose any path, the path of evil and pain or the path of God and peace." I asked him to show me the path of God and peace and help me to reach a place both of peace and wealth. He replied: "You couldn't be a servant of God and a servant of wealth simultaneously." "But," I said, "your financial life is so good." He replied: "Yes, but I am not a servant of wealth and I spend my time just praying to God and serving him." Then I agreed not to be servant of wealth and he taught me the way of God, to embrace true peace.

He was my teacher for weeks and months and he taught me how to obey such commands of God as: do not lie, do not fornicate, do not steal, do not backbite, etc. I thought there was a big problem with the lessons that he taught me. I doubted God's existence, because I was following his commands but I was suffering still.

I wanted to get rich internally and externally, and that was a surrendering and burning desire inside of me. I started to study the biographies of self-made millionaires and, to increase my physical and spiritual power in those hard times, I spent some time teaching Martial Arts to others, free of charge.

"Every problem and every unfortunate has a seed of success." (Napoleon Hill, *Think and Grow Rich*.)

When I started my research, I found those millionaires had some resources to initiate the success process that I didn't have then. A visa, nationality, permission to work, a language to communicate with, but I shared one thing with them, and that was inner ultimate energy such as all normal people have. If you put a burning desire into your unconscious, it will come true.

It needs just to find your goal inside of you. You have to examine yourself in a quiet place. And to do this you need to clear all the harmful things that are stored in your unconscious. And to clear them you need to be happy.

Do not worry about your scattered thoughts. Free them up. Do not divide them into good and bad. Do not worry about wasting time. Do not hurry. Be patient and believe your inner power. You will gradually learn how to put positive thoughts in your mind. Then they will nourish you by their power and will become a physical reality. Believe the power and persist in this process. I promise, if you follow this book and put the advice into action, you will achieve wealth and happiness and fulfilling relationships with your relatives.

CHAPTER 11

Poverty and wealth

Most of the important things in the world have been accomplished by people who have kept on trying when there seemed to be no hope at all.

One of the wrong ideas that is believed by working or middle class people is this: you have to suffer a lot and overcome many difficult obstacles to get rich. And this is a very disappointing idea. Some people believe moving toward wealth means they will recede from God, or they will not have any time to be with their family, or their relationships will collapse, as they will be always busy, becoming workaholics.

Other people think it is impossible to get rich because they haven't received an education, don't have any capital, are too old or exist within a bad environment. Unfortunately they missed the big discovery of Einstein: $E=mc2$.

Of course you are familiar with the equation. Please think about the theory for some moments. By focusing on it you will find out thoughts can become things. In this formula m represents mass of matter in inertia, E represents energy, and c represents the speed of light in a vacuum. This equation tells us that the mass of matter in inertia equals the inner energy of it. Or in other words, matter and energy are convertible to each other. It means if matter moves at the speed of light, it will turn to energy completely.

The history of humankind is full of proof that indicates all things started from just a thought, a thought that is nourished by a burning desire and faith and tolerance. Any thought or belief that tells you that you couldn't or shouldn't get rich is a false belief and it will cause you pain and unhappiness in life and blind you to life's blessings. As Australian entrepreneur Rachael Birmingham asserts: "The energy we put out is the energy we get back."

You should know there is more activity and tension in the lives of working and middle class families than in the lives of rich people. A few elite people injected these poisoned thoughts into the minds of poor people to keep their own power safe. They speak about disease, war, death, terrorism, murder, drugs, the bad economy and other miseries, and they give us some proof to make us believe them. They use religion, education, race, nationality and language to control the working and middle class population. And it is a lifetime programming of our minds for the sake of their personal benefits. But this programming does not work in the minds of everyone. Some people decide to take control of their minds and you are one of them because you are searching and you have decided to be true to your dreams. You don't allow anyone to steal your dreams or to put poisoned thoughts into your mind. You choose everything yourself. And you are aware of your authority to choose, you know you are responsible for your life and nothing can control you if you do not allow it.

The world has some defined principles. Nothing happens by chance. Believing in chance is one output of lack of knowledge. There are defined rules to getting rich. After learning and applying these rules you can become rich internally and externally. A lack of education or capital cannot prevent you from getting rich. Most self-made millionaires haven't any high academic education. Thomas Edison went to school just for three months, Henry Ford for less than six years, and Christopher Paolo Gardner was homeless in the 1980s. Randy Gage spent his childhood in poverty and became addicted to drugs and alcohol in adolescence.

Many of history's great and successful people-and many self-made millionaires-made their dreams come true despite having no money and little or no education, and even while facing the pressure of being ridiculed. Neither your age nor your environment-and indeed, nothing else, either-can prevent you from getting rich, whether internally or financially. Everything consists of energy.

CHAPTER 12

Intelligence and wealth

To manifest what you desire, you must have a clear picture of what you want in your mind and this picture must be chosen after study, research and analysis. According to Gilford and Christensen (*Creativity, Intelligence, and Personality* by Frank Barron and David M. Harrington) there is a meaningful relationship between intelligence and creativity only at a normal level of intelligence (an IQ of approximately 100) and above this level there is not any correlation between them. Thus high levels of intelligence are not necessary for being creative. According to my own research I believe that intelligence is not a necessity for getting rich. Mathematicians and physicians are not necessarily rich people. A normal level of intelligence such as most people have is sufficient.

Gardner's theory of multiple intelligences

Harvard psychologist Howard Gardner first outlined his theory of multiple intelligences in the book *Frames of Mind: The Theory of Multiple Intelligences*, published in 1983. It quickly became adopted as a useful model by which aspects of human intelligence, personality and behaviour could be learned and understood. Gardner's intelligences are different to intellectual capacity and provide a valuable alternative definition of the human experience, looking at it from a cognitive perspective.

The basis for Gardner's theory was the idea that everyone has a number of relatively independent mental faculties, or multiple intelligences. He says, 'A belief in a single intelligence assumes that we have one central, all-purpose computer – and it determines how well we perform in every sector of life. In contrast, a belief in multiple intelligences assumes that we have a number of relatively autonomous computers – one that computes linguistic information, another spatial information, another musical information, another information about other people, and so on.'

Gardner originally identified seven multiple intelligences, as follows:

- Linguistic; words and language
- Logical-Mathematical; logic and numbers
- Musical; music, sound, rhythm
- Bodily-Kinaesthetic; body movement control
- Spatial-Visual; images and space
- Interpersonal; other people's feelings
- Intrapersonal; self-awareness

Since then he has continued to develop and enhance the model and has put forward a further three possible additional intelligences:

- Naturalist; natural environment
- Spiritual / Existential; religion and "ultimate issues"
- Moral; ethics, humanity, value of life

The model provides a clear indication as to people's behavioural and working styles, and their natural strengths. Gardner suggests most people are strong in three types of intelligence and that these indicate not only a person's capabilities, but also the manner or method in which they prefer to learn. (Note that this has nothing to do with "learning styles", about which much has been written elsewhere; this merely involves playing to a person's natural abilities.) This allows them to take positive action to both further develop their strengths and also take action to address those areas where they perform less well.

For example, someone who is strong visually and weak linguistically will learn language better if things are explained using images to illustrate the meaning of the words used and, indeed, showing the words themselves.

A primary aspect of Gardner's reasoning is that intelligence is not able to be measured on a single, standard scale because each of the intelligences in our set will be different (stronger or weaker). Nevertheless, each has value. Aside from the fact it would be dull if we were all the same, we need people who are good at different things in order for society to function. Groups and teams are stronger for the diversity a range of intelligences brings, and it allows them greater capability, too.

Intelligence in schools and colleges is still generally measured on the basis of intelligence quotient, or IQ. On that basis, people are labelled "smart" or "stupid", and very many capable people are written off and made unhappy as a result.

But the simple fact is that many people who are successful in business were considered to be failures at school.

Gardner was one of the first people to assert that judging people against such a narrow and arbitrary definition of intelligence was wrong. People possess a vast range of capabilities; not all might be the sorts of things we traditionally value, such as the traditional three Rs (reading, writing and arithmetic) but not being good at those things doesn't make a person worthless or stupid. Someone with green fingers could be hugely successful in a horticultural environment and it wouldn't matter if he or she struggled with numbers; someone with a deep affinity with other people would be worth their weight in gold in a caring capacity, and the fact they were a slow reader wouldn't matter in the slightest.

So what does all this mean for you? Well, to fulfil your potential you need to play to your strengths. Not everyone needs to be good at science, maths and history and not everyone would become successful and rich as a result of going to university. It is very important that people know what type of intelligence they have as it is by doing things that are connected to that intelligence that they could become successful and live a fulfilled and happy life.

If you are strongest when it comes to music, for example, you will probably be miserable if you aim for a career in accountancy but if you are strongest when it comes to numbers, you might hate a job in sales.

There are jobs and businesses for all types of people, so aim to do what makes you most happy and least uncomfortable. If you need to be surrounded by people, look for opportunities that allow you to be; if you are shy and reserved, look for opportunities that allow you to succeed while nurturing that aspect of your nature.

It's a good idea to think long and hard about what you would do if you could choose absolutely anything in the world; giving yourself that kind of freedom will allow you to identify what it is that is your true purpose in life. So often we are on a treadmill from when we first start school to when we retire, graded and herded and pigeon-holed and assessed until we can't think any more about what it is that we want. We become slaves to the system and can see no way to break free. For many people their worst nightmare is to lose their job, but many, when you talk to them about it six months or a year or more later, will tell you that it was the best thing that ever happened to them. Why? First, because it forced them to take stock and to start making positive choices about what they wanted to do next in their life and second, because it gave them the time and space in which to do that.

So please do take the time to consider what you are best at, to identify where it is that your intelligence lies. For those who prefer to take a test, a number of free tests based on Gardner's model may be found online.

CHAPTER 13

Self-control

*"You have power over your mind - not outside events. Realize this,
and you will find strength."*

Marcus Aurelius

To become rich or to achieve any other success in your life you have to
gain full control of your mind. There are lots of harmful programmes
recorded in your unconscious and they affect your thoughts and your
behaviour.

You may drink, smoke, eat fast food, eat a lot and avoid exercise,
or you may be jealous, arrogant, and revengeful, or you may blame the
environment or other people for your failures. You may not have a good
relationship with your wife/husband or your children, and you may not
trust people, or be frightened or disappointed by them. You may not like
your job, you may be poisoned by a political belief or a religion, or you
may believe you have to die for your homeland, or you may be trapped
by some other form of negativity: disappointment, humiliation,
helplessness, weakness or any bad feeling that makes you dissatisfied.
Even if you don't have any bad feelings, you may be trapped in a
miserable life and suffer from limiting beliefs, or only learn things based
on another's injected thoughts. There are lots of rich people suffering
from being under another's control. But in this book I will teach you a
path to achieve peace and wealth simultaneously.

The difference between a worried rich person and a peaceful rich
person is related to mind control. When your thoughts are in harmony
with the rules of the universe you can achieve both wealth and inner
peace. A person who has no control over his thoughts is unable to
perform wisely; he is like a robot that some other person or the
environment controls. Actually he is no different from a dead person.

But you are a human being and you can choose life or death, and I am sure everyone wants to have a real life.

But remember, to achieve this kind of life full of wealth, bliss and peace, you have to pay the cost, just like many others, and just like me when I learnt and applied this principle many years ago, and then received bliss and happiness in return. I was alone, I was ridiculed, I suffered from hunger, I was accused, I saw my family's difficulties, but I kept on.

CHAPTER 14

Become yourself

In this chapter I want to share one of the greatest secrets of the world with you.

As mentioned before, you need to open up your mind and have a burning desire and strong decision to step onto the path of success. If you are not ready you will hate this chapter and call these writings evil and damn me. You will act just as your controllers want you to. They taught you to hate people like me. They don't want you to be happy and rich. Perhaps you think you have enemies and your enemies are a group of people that grab your money, spirit, honour and happiness, and you have to fight to eliminate them. But don't; that would be wrong. You have just one enemy and that is you, because you agree to be in the control of others, whether that is intentional or unintentional. There is no difference. If you do not understand this chapter it will cost you dear. I want to share a big secret with you and that is: you have to be bad to reach success and happiness. Very bad!

Open your eyes, or if you can't, open up your ears. This secret is absolutely in front of your eyes and its voice is heard everywhere. You just need to analyse the lives of great men and women from the initial stages. It is also true about groups, organizations, companies and wealthy and powerful countries. All of them started from the same point. Do not be tricked by their current status; when they started, their steps to success were considered to be very bad in the eyes of others, very bad, stupid and foolish.

You need to accept that you won't be able to satisfy everyone around you. So don't try.

Be yourself and only live to satisfy yourself. Learn to love yourself as you are, love all your thoughts and actions and don't label them as either good and bad. Accept yourself and don't try to be what others expect you to be or like to see from you.

When exactly you become yourself, begin showing some love to yourself, enjoy your thoughts and don't judge them or label them, then you will be FREE.

You will become calmer and happier than ever.

The fact is, at that time there are also going to be people from all different backgrounds and associated to a variety of backgrounds who will reject you.

Society and governments don't want you to have the ultimate freedom and therefore it might not be easy for you to choose this path.

But when you accept this without giving it any specific meaning and feelings of guilt, you have managed to break the steel chains that have been holding you back from real success.

Remember that history is full of great men and women who were humiliated by the public, but after an insufferable period, or in many cases after their death, the truth about what they said did become apparent.

Do not be afraid to be yourself, even if you have thought that becoming what you truly are is bad.

Because the only way to become successful is to be yourself.

Don't believe in God until you become an atheist first

When you believe in God you face lots of difficulties. If you believe in God you might assume this part of the book is sinister, but the point is that people take away your control in the name of God, Satan, heaven, hell, good, bad, nationality, country, skin colour, race, etc.

An absence of the external and physical existence of God causes you to follow other humans that claim to have come from him or to know him. They teach you lots of valuable things but at the same time in that salubrious water there is one drop of a poison that will take your life.

In the name of God they ask you to pay money, to work for free, to risk your life and money in some cases, and some want you to be an obedient sheep, don't ask questions and just believe them and be obedient.

You may also say that lots of people that believe in God are wealthy.

No, no, no, don't make that mistake. They are not really wealthy because the price of accumulating that money is by fooling others, poverty and the blood of human beings. They are never going to tell you that deep in their heart they don't believe in God.

Religious leaders are those who rape our children and take our life and money in the name of God and his services.

If you really believe in God, you can only say that when you experience atheism first. The very first step toward this would be erasing all the beliefs that have been injected into your mind and soul, then without being under any influence, with a conscious mind and a pure soul, search for the truth about God.

Don't follow religion

If you believe in God's existence never follow any religion.

The person who follows a specific religion without any doubts and easily will be under the control of a religious leader. In such a case he will have no control over his life any more.

A religious person will let leaders think for him and decide on behalf of him. They make people feel guilty and in many cases this will lead to depression and anxiety.

And it's interesting to remember that history shows that the biggest amount of killing, stealing, plunders and crimes were committed by religions and in the name of their Gods.

You might ask me why have you put quotes from the Bible in your book? Of course, there are informative things in religious books. However, you will be trapped and captured exactly when, instead of reading them as instructive books, you look at them as books that were sent from God. You must learn to recognize a drop of poison in a glass of pure water. You will eventually learn this by being happy, calm and without resistance.

Choose your goal without fear

Make a choice from a range of possibilities and don't doubt the path to your goal. Be sure that you will get there. In the path of achieving any goals, there are difficulties and temporary defeats you will face along the way.

Don't doubt that you may have chosen the wrong path because however small or big your goal is and even if you change direction on the way to achieve your targets, you will face some difficulties. At such time all the negative thoughts could attack you and show you that you won't get there, but you should not listen.

Sometimes you can't even see or imagine what would happen next and all the forces are against you, but still you should not stop and still you need to go forward.

It doesn't matter whether you are going fast or slow, only that you are moving forward in your dream or in the physical world, you only need to move and go forward toward your ultimate goal without any uncertainty and doubt.

Being certain about something means that you sincerely believe in achieving your goal and this is a very important law for becoming successful in life.

Don't just think of the result

People usually, after choosing an objective, begin thinking of whether they can attain it or not.

They keep thinking if:

- I achieve my ambitions I will be the happiest person on the earth.
- I obtain that goal I will be forever in peace, and etc.

For clearing this subject I use a simple example:

Imagine someone wants to go from point A to point B (his goal) in five years' time.

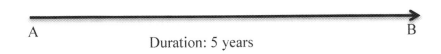

A   B

Duration: 5 years

In the whole five years that he is moving toward his goal he is only thinking of getting to point B. After passing the five years in this way there are a few possibilities; he might think:

1. I am so happy and grateful to achieve my goal.
2. I have achieved my goal but I am not happy with this.
3. This is not what I was aiming to get and I think I should continue toward the next goal.
4. I have not achieved my goal. (And he believes he's been defeated and feels hopeless.)
5. Etc.

We can add more to these but the point is in such a case, the person has given five years of his beautiful life and lost them to get to his goal.

Maybe in that five years he didn't enjoy eating food, didn't spend enough time with his family, didn't have time to lie on the ground and watch the blue sky, didn't have time to go to nature and breathe deep, didn't get time to sit and talk to a stranger, didn't have time to learn new skills, maybe he was too busy to even dance with his partner, forgot to wear colourful clothes, didn't sing loudly in the shower, enjoy gardening and many more things besides.

Some people miss all the enjoyment and pleasure of life to get to their goal and then they wonder why they still aren't happy. Some say this is the price of this goal. They basically scarify every day of that period to get to their goal and this is the biggest mistake you can make.

I know people who work so hard that they never get a chance to see their kids or play with them. But then they feel pride because they have sent the kids to a private school or they are satisfied to see their children's graduation. But then those kids will never be totally happy because you are their parents and when they needed to talk to you or get your advice you were not there to help them, or they may even feel sorry for themselves when they hear that the closest friend of their best mate is their dad/mum.

You know what, you must learn to enjoy each year, month, day, hour, minute and even each second. All of the universe's beauties should be included in your goal, without them the goal is nothing.

In the same time that you move from point A to point B you should enjoy every little thing on the way. Learn to love every second of this path and assume every step of the way is a goal.

When you chose a goal, the success wouldn't be achieving point B after five years. You should enjoy every step of the way and enjoying every minute of this path is called the ultimate success.

In your direction to success whether it's easy or hard you should enjoy it and keep learning.

Rule of silence

Silence is one of the biggest and most powerful ways for being successful.

The person who doesn't understand the rules of success and is on his way to success is like a young plant about to grow or a newborn baby who needs to be protected.

By talking too much about your goals and targets you will attract negative thoughts, even your family or friends might feel pity for you because of the impossible or difficult way that you might have started and they keep talking about it with you.

Negative thought will attack your dreams so hard that you won't have any strength left to develop them. Even if they are supporting you

45

and tell you that you are capable of doing that kind of stuff, again they will not be positive because fear will be created inside you that you might be unsuccessful and let them down.

And fear of losing (being unsuccessful) is one of the most dangerous toxins for being successful.

So whenever you have a dream or goal in your mind, chase it up in silence and just mention it to people whom you need help from in that area.

Rule of being alone

Everything is born from the heart of solitude.

Being alone is one of the things that government, religion and society will steal from you.

You being alone is too dangerous for those who try to control your mind and that's because by you being independent you will find out the secret, which is you are being controlled.

In solitude you will be close to who you really are and you can see the environment around you clearly.

Your dreams have to be born in solitude and without any effects (influence).

Government, religion and society made people scared of being and feeling alone.

Have you ever wondered why, whenever you are alone, you will come up with some kind of excuse just to run away from that! You would watch TV, read the newspaper, talk on the phone with someone, use the Internet, the computer, go out, and so many other things.

You will run away from yourself without realizing it and that's because they programmed your mind so they can think and decide instead of you.

I remember the day after finding out the truth I was feeling pity for myself, but today I feel pity for those who are still being controlled like a puppet.

To be successful and gain true wealth with peace you must be yourself and be independent.

Assign a few hours every day or at least a few hours in the week for being just alone.

When you're alone think about yourself. Be calm so your dreams can be born and make plans for your goals.

Never ever run away from solitude.

Solitude is the best and most precious friend of human beings.

CHAPTER 15

Recognition

Self-awareness is one of the keys to getting rich. But what does it mean? How can we achieve self-awareness? Let me start from the moment of birth. This is not only a physical birth! It is an awakened force and a powerful perception that is called many names, such as spirit or energy, and each of these births is unique and different from others.

Self-awareness is the ability to see how your thoughts, behaviours and beliefs affect not only others, but also yourself. Developing self-awareness involves taking a long, hard look in the mirror and being honest about what you see. It takes courage to do this as it involves admitting that you have been wrong or have acted badly at times, but only by being honest with yourself can you develop self-awareness and use that knowledge to improve and to be successful.

Once you know your weaknesses, you can look for patterns in your behaviour and your reactions to certain triggers and situations. If those patterns and reactions are negative and harmful to you, then you can begin to change them. You have to do this consciously; many of your reactions are programmed into you and are an element of external control.

Pay close attention to your thoughts. Remember, everything starts from thought; thoughts become reality. Will your thoughts help you succeed and make you happy? Or will they hold you back and keep you from living the life you desire and deserve?

You must be willing to make changes. If you keep doing the same things in the same way then nothing will ever change; success will be impossible. Even when you start to get results, remember that it is always possible to fine tune your performance so you can become stronger and better and even more successful.

Self-awareness allows you to live a fully conscious life and to be the real you; it gives you control over your life and your mind so that you aren't at the mercy of external forces. It's the difference between

47

blundering along and repeating the same mistakes and taking charge of your life to create your own destiny.

CHAPTER 16

The universal laws

I believe that the wisest teacher and mentor I had was life itself. Sometimes I had to go down the longest and hardest path that you can imagine to gain knowledge and learn those lessons, but then I found wise mentors whom I have learned from. Our thoughts determine our destiny and we are able to control our thoughts.

Most people nowadays are aware of the Law of Attraction, but are unaware that it is not the only one. In fact, there are a number of universal laws that seem somehow to have been overlooked by the general population. Depending on who you talk to, you might be told of seven, eleven, twelve or more, and while you may argue that you know some of them, being aware of them, and understanding and putting what you learned into action, are two very different things.

I want to pay attention here to twelve lesser-known universal laws:

The Law of Success
The Law of Thinking
The Law of Supply
The Law of Attraction
The Law of Receiving
The Law of Increase
The Law of Compensation
The Law of Non-Resistance
The Law of Forgiveness
The Law of Sacrifice
The Law of Obedience
The Law of Cause and Effect
We will take a closer look at each of those now.

The Law of Success

The battle for success is half-won when you know absolutely what it is that you want. When someone knows what they want and have made up their mind to get it, whatever the cost, then it is all over bar the shouting.

Just focus on that for a moment. Once someone knows what they want to be successful in, that success is as good as theirs.

Now ask yourself this: when was the last time I was very successful at something and it made me feel bad? I can guarantee it has never happened. Success always results in good feelings.

Now I want you to get a piece of paper and a pen-or use a portable digital device, whatever's easiest-and just take few minutes to think of all the successes you've enjoyed in your life. It doesn't matter how old you were at the time, or how long ago it was; it can be anything, ever. Next I want you to select maybe half a dozen of these real-life successful stories and write them down. Read them over and you'll probably find that you're smiling; they certainly won't make you feel bad, that's for certain.

You should carry the piece of paper (or your phone, or whatever other device you may have used) with you and take it out frequently to read your list of successes. Do this at least twice every day for the next three-month. Why? Because you want to activate the mindset that brought on your successes. It was the same for each of them: you expected something and you got it.

The Law of Thinking

This is hugely important. What are you thinking about? Be honest, because through the power of your thoughts, you have to create the love, the happiness, the wealth, whatever it is that you want; you've got to create it first within yourself. As the Victorian philosopher William James said, "We live our life as it is imagined in our mind." Everything starts with your thoughts. To change the reality, first you need to change your thoughts. If you want immediate results, you need to begin thinking of all of the things that you need and want in your life. Every night before sleeping think of those things that you want and I promise you that they begin to appear in no time. Remember that universe will attract to you whatever thought you keep thinking of so, be aware of your thought.

The Law of Supply

The next law is the Law of Supply. Basic economics has familiarised us with supply and demand, but this is a case of demand and supply.

Bob Proctor says, "There's a phase of the law known as demand and supply which is found in every department of life. What we can learn from that is that when we demand something, the supply will be there. What it means to us is that we have to tell the universe exactly what we want. We must demand it! The universe takes those ideas that you impress upon the universal mind and brings whatever it is you have thought into being-you can demand everything that you need, but you must expect wholeheartedly to receive it. You've got to see it coming. It's demand and supply; it's not supply and demand. There is never a lack of supply; whatever you demand will come to you."

The Law of Attraction

This is the most widely known law, the law that underpins *The Secret*. Emerson said, "See how the masses of men worry themselves into nameless graves while here and there a great, unselfish soul forgets himself into immortality."

When you see nothing but the good that you can do, you will set up a very strong attractive force. You must know and be very clear about what you want to attract but remember, if you're asking for something big, then you must render a big service. When you embrace the idea of putting that out, you're going to start to attract.

You must understand that the image you visualise sets up the vibration and the vibration dictates what you attract. If you visualise what it is you want and expect it to come into your life, then it will. You'll get some things that you weren't expecting and you're not necessarily going to know everything that you'll need; your job is to believe that everything you need will come to you. Expect something good. Expect a miracle. And you'll invoke the Law of Attraction.

The Law of Receiving

Receiving is an interesting concept. In the Christian Bible in the New Testament, Luke 6:38, it says, "Give and it shall be given unto you-good measure, pressed down, and shaken together, and running over." In other words, if we lock into giving, we're going to receive more than we will ever, ever need.

Give willingly and receive graciously. You must be gracious and open to receive. Understand this: you are the highest form of creation on the planet. You deserve all the good that life offers.

51

The Law of Increase

When you're praised for doing something, you open up and come alive, you can't help but smile, your whole demeanour changes. If you're criticized, you contract, you avoid eye contact and you withdraw. You get defensive.

What we can learn from this is that praise is a marvellous tool and one that we can use to our advantage. We should be alert to what's going on around us so that whenever we get the chance, we can offer praise. We want to praise everything we do; it's praise that causes everything to grow-even the plants in our homes. Love them, send them good energy.

Take a few minutes to think of who does good things around you. Now consider how you can praise them. The caveat is that you've got to be sincere; insincere praise-flattery-won't work, because the energy is generated inside, not outside.

The Law of Compensation

Many of us are not at all happy with our compensation-that is, with what we receive. If we study the Law of Compensation, however, everything can change.

The Law of Compensation involves three elements: the amount of money you earn is in direct ratio to first, the need for what you do; secondly, your ability to do it; and thirdly, the difficulty involved in replacing you. That's three different points. The most important of these is the second one, it's your ability. It's how you serve others. How good are you at doing what you're doing? If there is a need for it, and if you become really good at it, you're going to be fairly difficult to replace.

It's said the cemetery is full of indispensable people, but it is undeniable that some people are earning an awful lot more money than others. If you want to increase your income, really study the Law of Compensation. Decide right now that you're going to become so much better at what you do.

Take a little time to consider two or three things you can do, beginning today, to become more effective at what you do. That's the first step towards boosting your compensation.

The Law of Non-Resistance

Pay attention, because this is important: whatever you resist, will persist. This takes a bit of thinking about, it seems almost counter-intuitive.

If you resist a situation, you'll always have it with you. If you try to run away from it, it follows you like a shadow. If you've ever been on a diet you'll understand this; you're trying to eat less or eat differently, but all you can think about is food. If you're trying to resist chocolate, chocolate is what's on your mind.

If you ignore the difficulty of the condition and fearlessly work around it, however, you will find a time when that difficulty will have been absorbed and removed. Accept the condition as some evidence of good. Look for that good, and being acceptable to it, more and more evidence of it appears.

The idea is that if there is bad stuff coming your way, you don't resist it, you don't fight it-you just let it go. It doesn't mean that you have to become a doormat or get used or beaten up by it. Just don't resist it.

Try it. When someone is angry or upset and is shouting accusations at you, say a prayer for them, bless them, send them good, positive energy. That way, instead of becoming attuned to their angry vibration, you create your own beautifully harmonious vibration. Ultimately, that will attract nothing but good to you.

So, to recap, the Law of Non-Resistance says don't resist; whatever you resist, will persist. I accept that this can be tricky to fully understand; certainly I had to study it for quite a while before I really got my head around it, but if you put the time in to get to grips with it fully, it will pay off in spades.

Just think for a moment; what have you been resisting? What is dogging your footsteps and halting your progress? Whatever it might be, stop it. Let it go and be calm. You'll find it works like pure magic.

The Law of Forgiveness

This is another tricky one. The things we hear as we grow up are "stick up for yourself", "get your own back", "don't back down". But that doesn't do us any good. That puts us into a bad vibration. What does do us good is to forgive.

To forgive means to let go of completely; to abandon. If someone is doing something that is wrong, whether it's something that's unlawful, or they're trying to hurt you, let it go. The second you start to try and get even with them you put your mind in the wrong vibration. If you're doing something wrong, the law is going to see that you get it back. The universe gives everything back, equal and opposite.

Forgiveness is a very personal thing. If someone does something wrong and you forgive them, you don't do it for their benefit, you do it for your benefit. You get rid of the conflict, you get rid of the bad thoughts in your mind, you allow yourself to move into a beautiful vibration.

If you don't forgive, you're going to be battling the concept forever, and it is a concept. Let it go. Try it; once you get the hang of it, you'll really reap the benefits.

Take a few minutes to think about what's been bothering you lately and forgive it. It might be a person, or an organization, or it could be a situation. Whatever it is, forgive it. Let it go.

Put yourself in a very relaxed state and imagine yourself tying a helium balloon to whatever it is. See it float away and wave it off with forgiveness in your heart. As you watch it float away in your mind's eye, you'll realize that you're the one who is feeling lighter as you no longer have that weighing you down.

The Law of Sacrifice

You have to create a space for the good that you desire. The Law of Sacrifice is very closely connected to the Vacuum Law of Prosperity. Randy Gage tells us: "The universe cannot put good into your hand, until you let go of what you are holding in it. You are surrounded by good everywhere. The only lack is the lack in your mind. Open your mind to receive prosperity, create a vacuum to hold it, and you will attract it." In other words, you must create a space for the good that you desire.

The Law of Obedience

Whatever law you obey is going to serve you. The most important thing is to know what to obey. We've been talking about the Law of Forgiveness, the Law of Sacrifice, the Law of Attraction. If we obey these laws-abide by the strategies, develop the mental discipline to follow them-then those laws are going to serve us. But since most of us have not been raised to be obedient to those laws, we violate them. We become obedient to things that are doing us no good at all. Let's obey the Law and the Law will serve us.

The Law of Cause and Effect

Everything happens for a reason and every action has a consequence. The choices you make have results, it doesn't matter whether they are conscious or unconscious. The Law of Cause and Effect will work the same for everyone and will always have a corresponding outcome.

This law is very different from the other laws; this is about what you put out, which will provoke an appropriate result.

54

I have seen many hard working people who put out everything they have to achieve their targets. The only thing that they forget to do is to follow the right footsteps. If you really have the desire to be successful in your chosen field, then you must find and study those people who are already successful in that field. Learn everything about them, read the books they read, get to know them better and follow them. This law certifies that if they became successful through taking those actions, you will, too if you do the same things.

About the laws

These laws were not invented by me and I do not want to persuade you by them. This is a mechanism of the universe, this is a rule, and it will be forever so whether we are aware of it or not.

Do not waste your time with questions such as, where did they come from? Or where did I come from? Or where do I go to? Humankind has thought about these questions for thousands of years and given thousands of answers to them with thousands of religions. Just focus on HOW. How can I achieve inner and outer wealth by applying these rules? This process begins with the things that make you happy and peaceful and make your life more beautiful. You can answer your questions when you are at peace with yourself and then you will perceive these rules and move faster on the path toward wealth. You are here to live, to find out the meaning of life.

"Life is a woman. Try to understand life and you will become a mess. Forget all about understanding. Just live it and you will understand it. The understanding is not going to be intellectual or theoretical; the understanding is going to be total." (Osho Diamond: *A New Vision for the New Millennium*.)

There is just one way to live; control your mind and become aware of your inner world. You need to cleanse your unconscious of negative beliefs and believe this rule: a human being can achieve anything he or she wants. Do not say no. Do not lie to yourself.

CHAPTER 17

Steps to follow to gain wealth

Nikola Tesla said: "Every living being is an engine geared to the wheelwork of the universe. Though seemingly affected only by its immediate surrounding, the sphere of external influence extends to infinite distance."

What this means for us is that we can use our knowledge of the laws of the universe to create the reality that we choose for ourselves, and we can choose to be rich.

As I said near the start of the book, a rich person is a person who lives in full peace, has financial and spiritual power, and brings happiness and bliss to the lives of others.

You must believe in yourself, you must open up your mind and have a burning desire and strong decision to step onto the path of success.

Remember the two rules I told you about; the rule of silence and the rule of being alone.

Silence is important because by talking too much about your goals and targets you will attract negative thoughts. Keep your own counsel; beautiful things happen when you distance yourself from the negative.

Being alone is important because to be successful and gain true wealth with peace you must be calm. This allows your dreams to be born and gives you the chance to make plans for your goals.

Remember the laws of the universe:

The Law of Success
The Law of Thinking
The Law of Supply
The Law of Attraction
The Law of Receiving
The Law of Increase
The Law of Compensation

The Law of Non-Resistance

The Law of Forgiveness

The Law of Sacrifice

The Law of Obedience

The Law of Cause and Effect

Follow them and use them to your own advantage. All you have to do is ask and your every desire can be fulfilled.

Next I have for you a simple two stage structure to follow to ensure your chances of success.

Structure for success

Stage 1: Prepare your mind

Remember that Raymond Holliwell, in *Working With the Law*, said:

"Life, with all its attributes of good, is something that doesn't just happen to touch a fortunate few. It is something you must create. It is something you must plan, mentally picture and think about. You who are seeking love, fortune, happiness, success must understand that it is not something you can find. You cannot buy it; you can never borrow it from another. No one can give it to you; you must create it within yourself."

"Now our method is not manipulating two powers, good and evil. We've got to create. The mind force is creating continually like fertile soil. Nature does not differentiate between the seed of the weed and that of the flower. She produces and causes both seeds to grow."

So for the best chances of success, make sure your thoughts are positive. Whatever it is that you want; you must first create it within yourself. This doesn't mean if you get annoyed about something that you can't let off steam, it just means that the majority of your thoughts should be positive.

There are some things you can do to help achieve this and to get in the right mindset. For a start, remember every day to look at your list of successes at least once. Read about people who have already achieved what you want to achieve; think what that must feel like; if you can, do what they did; focus on the positive.

Be grateful for the good things you already have. These might feel like precious few at the moment, but I'm sure there will be something for which you feel true gratitude, whether it's your partner, your children, your pet or even the view from your window. At least once a day focus on that feeling of gratitude and put that out there to the universe.

Consciously become more self-aware; it will help you to eliminate bad habits and cultivate better ones, and to avoid making the same mistakes over and over again. It will also help you to see whether something you believe to be true really is your own belief or is a result of external programming; be yourself, don't be a puppet.

Praise people whenever you can; look for opportunities to make them feel good and it will raise the vibration for everyone.

Don't resist bad things; let them go. Have you ever walked into a room where two people are arguing? You can feel the bad vibration as soon as you walk through the door; neither will give up or give in and the whole atmosphere is poisoned as a result. Don't allow that to affect you; forgive, offer a blessing and walk away.

Once your mind is prepared, move on to the second stage.

Stage 2: Ask the universe for what you want
There are five steps to this stage of the process, as follows:

Step 1: establish what you want
Step 2: write it down
Step 3: set aside time to visualize having it
Step 4: expect to receive what you have asked for
Step 5: don't give up; keep believing, keep anticipating
Let's take a closer look at them.

Step 1: establish what you want
This is where you focus on exactly what you want so that when you ask for it, you get it. I can't tell you how important this is; remember, the universe doesn't judge you or question you, it just gives to you what you ask it to give to you.

Some years ago a young woman asked the universe for her car loan to be paid off; shortly afterwards she was in a crash, her car was written off and the insurance company paid off the loan. That wasn't exactly what she wanted to happen! Had she been more specific and said, for example, "I want to own my car outright," then the outcome would very likely have been different.

Give this some thought; take time to establish exactly what it is that you want, so that when you ask the universe, you get it.

Step 2: write it down
Once you know what you want, visualize it and then write down exactly what success will look like, or even draw it, if you can, so that you can give the universe the clearest possible request, resulting in a good outcome for you.

If you want to attract a certain sum of money, write yourself a cheque for that amount. You don't have to use a real one (although you can, if you wish) you can just sketch one out showing the Bank of the Abundant Universe is to pay that sum to you.

If you want to attract an object, whether it's a new phone or a house, get a picture of the one you want (or one like it).

It's a great idea to keep a notebook in which you have written the details, drawn the pictures or stuck the images of the things you have asked for.

Step 3: set aside time to visualize having it

Every day, set aside some time to connect with the universe and visualize having what it is you have asked for. Use your notebook to keep the image clear; imagine how you will feel now that whatever it is you have asked for is yours. Say it out loud, if you can. "I am a millionaire; thank you, abundant universe," for example, or, "I drive an Aston Martin; thank you, abundant universe."

Do this morning and night.

Before you start you might want to read your list of successes to get into the right mindset and, as part of the process, you might want to express your gratitude for the good things in your life. Raise the vibration; remember that like attracts like.

Step 4: expect to receive what you have asked for

Remember when you were small and you were looking forward to your birthday? You were in a state of high anticipation because you knew good things were coming your way.

Aim to replicate that mindset; you have asked the universe for something and the universe will deliver. You don't have to worry about a thing, you just have to look forward to receiving what you asked for in abundance.

Step 5: don't give up; keep believing, keep anticipating

If it takes a little while to get what you want, don't despair. Remember that while the seed has been sown in fertile ground, some seeds germinate quickly, but others take a little longer. Whatever you do, don't give up, keep believing that the universe will deliver, keep anticipating the wonderful feeling you will have when you receive your gifts. Have faith that your harvest will be bountiful.

Stage 3: Find and read great books

Find books that help you achieve your goals. Through reading, you expose yourself to new spiritual, intellectual and scientific things, new information, new ways to achieve success and new ways to solve problems.

I'm going to introduce you to a book that I believe is one of the best books I've ever read. I've recommended it to a lot of people and it's changed a lot of lives. It's called, "Think and Grow Rich", by Napoleon Hill. It's a phenomenal book.

Stage 4: Find good teachers

I believe that each of us can be the best teacher for ourselves because in the deepest part of our being we have the greatest teacher of all times. Since we have been programmed and controlled from the first moment of birth until now, making connection with that inner teacher inside us would be hard. It takes us lots of time and requires us to once again reprogramme ourselves and take control of our own lives. In that situation a good teacher like Bob Proctor could help you traverse your path to your purposes easier and quicker.

Next steps

Spend time every day affirming your requests in line with the universal laws. Practice using them and cultivate the right mindset to manifest whatever it is you want. Develop the mental discipline to obey the laws.

Also, learn as much as you can about the laws and principles. Read widely, both about the laws and about the sort of people you want to be like. Set up the right vibration to attract what is that you want.

Keep a record of what you have asked for and when, and what the outcome was. As you get better at this and enjoy more successes, you can use the information in your notebook to help raise your vibration and achieve more successes.

Remember that you don't just need to use this for the big things in life; you can start off by asking for small things – a seat on the train at rush hour or a table at a busy restaurant when you ring up at the last minute to book for a celebratory meal.

And that leads into another thing; celebrate your successes. Have a nice meal and raise a glass and thank the universe for delivering what you ordered from it. Always remember; a life of abundance and comfort is your birthright; claim it as your own and enjoy every minute.

CHAPTER 18

Follow your dream

As I mentioned earlier, it's a good idea to read about people who have overcome the odds and become successful; if they could do it, then so can you. History is full of real stories about people who turn their destiny from misery to bliss just by using a burning desire. History never lies. I cite just some examples here.

Oprah Winfrey
Oprah Winfrey was born into poverty in 1954 to an unwed teenage mother. However, poverty did not prevent her from becoming successful and she was named one of the "100 Most Influential People of the 20th Century" by Time magazine.

Oprah has many business interests; she is a partner in Oxygen Media, Inc., a cable channel and interactive network presenting programming designed primarily for women. She also publishes two magazines.

J.K. Rowling
In 2004, Forbes named Rowling as the first person to become a US dollar billionaire by writing books, the second-richest female entertainer and the 1,062nd richest person in the world. In February 2013 she was assessed as the 13th most powerful woman in the United Kingdom by Woman's Hour on BBC Radio 4.

Li Ka Shing
You may think you cannot become a rich and strong personality because you lack an education, or you miss your father and you haven't got any support. But let me tell you about Li Ka Shing:

Li Ka-Shing is one of the richest and most powerful men in the world. He is the boss of the conglomerate Hutchison Whampoa, Cheung Kong Holdings and Watson Group. The business mogul is the ninth richest person in the world with a net worth of approximately 25.5 billion dollars (according to Forbes).

Ka-Shing is also a distinguished philanthropist; he has pledged to give one third of his wealth to charitable institutions and philanthropist developments all over the world.

Ralph Lauren

Lauren never graduated from college, never went to fashion school, and would certainly not have seemed destined to head a global multi-billion-dollar luxury-goods company. He was born in 1939 in the Bronx, New York, to an immigrant family from Belarus who struggled to make ends meet. While at high school he acquired a taste for expensive high-quality clothing, and began selling ties to his classmates to finance the passion. After serving in the US army in the early 60s, he worked as a salesman in a clothing store and started making and selling his own ties, again on the side.

In 1967, he took a loan of fifty thousand dollars to launch his brand, which he named Polo-not because he had ever played the sport, but because of what the name symbolised for him. "It was the sport of kings," Lauren tells evancarmichael.com. "It was glamorous, sexy, and international."

His ties caused a small revolution: they were different in fabric, width, and colour, and rapidly became the indispensable accessory for men looking for up-to-date elegance. He says; "At the time men expressed themselves through their ties. A beautiful tie made it possible simultaneously to express quality, taste, and style."

Last words

It would take thousands and thousands of pages to tell the story of all the self-made millionaires in history. Great men and women make their dreams come true. They never give up and, despite facing difficulties, they move ahead until they succeed.

By following the advice in this book you, too, can enjoy success and you can become one of them.

Good luck, and follow your dream.

EPILOGUE

The little boy was only three years old when one day he heard terrible screams and continuous shooting from outside the house. He didn't know that the soldiers had come to kill his dad. He didn't know that in their city being open-minded was a crime and the price was death.

Without having any question or answer in his mind, he reached the front window and looked outside, then suddenly a soldier started shooting at the room that he was in. His dad jumped in front of him, he was just like a shield, he defended him and saved his son from the bullets. In the same moment the bullet that was aimed to kill the little boy went right into dad's arm.

The government's guards came to kill the dad because he didn't want to follow their God and also he didn't want to walk the path that they were recommending, and the reason for his disobedience was that he was a free man and very open minded. They came to his house to kill him; they didn't care about his children and wife that were home at that time.

Even though the dad was badly injured and was bleeding, he didn't want to stay at home and risk his family's lives, hence he went into the yard and as he was running away he was shot in the back.

He was very strong and was still breathing, then one of the soldiers put his boot on his throat and pressed.

The children were looking at their brave dad and at the soldiers that had been controlled by government and religion and who were transformed into murderers so that killing innocent people was their honor.

Just like all the soldiers in the world they were puppets that were manipulated by governments and religious leaders.

When their father was dead, his children felt the pain of being orphans, they became poor and began to be avoided by others.

Three years later their mother was forced into an unwanted marriage because of the numerous problems and difficulties she faced.

The stepfather was beating the little boy with his belt, wood, his hand and so on in the name of pedagogics. He had been beaten so much that most of the time his little body was all bruised and bleeding. His mother tried to defend her little boy but unfortunately, the stepdad was a lot stronger than her. All these tortures and torments continued for several years. The stepdad scared the little boy, humiliated him, and asked him to work like a slave; when he failed to obey him, he would beat the little boy.

The life of poverty, the death of his father, having a cruel stepdad and so on were all taking away his childhood dreams and telling him that he would never achieve his little dreams.

Regardless of the pains and torments, the boy had a huge soul; he was God and his steel knees wouldn't break under those tortures. Until one day another painful strike hit his big soul and little mind. The pain was so massive that he could not believe it. On that day his little sister told him that for several years she had been sexually abused by their stepdad. In that moment he felt that he lost a great power. At that time he didn't know that the minds of the majority of people were hunted by the Jewel wasp and he couldn't understand that the problem was not his stepdad, rather it was the wrong system that caused pains like this in societies. This is what's happening all over the world, but some governments are determined to hide them.

He had pain because he learnt that is something common and normal. However, he stood up again and regained his lost power.

He remembered a delightful story;

There once was a farmer that was walking down the trail when he discovered an eagle's nest with two eggs in it. He took one of the eggs and placed it in a nearby prairie chicken nest.

When the egg hatched, the little eagle thought he was a prairie chicken. Prairie chickens stay on the ground and eat only worms and grubs. So, as the eagle grew, he ate nothing but worms and grubs, and he walked around with the other prairie chickens. Just like prairie chickens, the eagle was afraid of rats and foxes.

One day when he was very old, he looked up in the sky and saw some eagles soaring high above. He asked one of the prairie chickens, "Since I was little I have always seen those birds, what is their name? How can they fly up there while we are down here eating worms and grubs?"

The prairie chicken answered, "They are the eagles, they can do that because they are lords of the air; we venerate them as living symbols of power, freedom, and transcendence. Man for many years has taken eagles to be a symbol of beauty, bravery, courage, honour, pride, determination and grace. However, we must stay down here. We are prairie chickens and that is what we do."

So, the eagle spent the rest of his life flying very little and eating worms and grubs, just because he was told that was all he could do. On the last day of his life he told the prairie chickens that he had always dreamed of being an eagle and they were the last words that he said.

The little boy grew up and he became the master of poetry and drawing, and a champion. He learnt to stretch his boundaries and try new things rather than focusing on his weaknesses and listening to the limitations that others put on him.

He knew that his seed wouldn't grow in that desert anymore. He was the eagle in the chicken nest, but he didn't want the same outcome as the eagle had. Hence he began his journey; he faced the poverty and hunger, and sought wealth. He learned about the secret of controlling the mind.

He didn't want to become the old eagle among the chickens. He didn't want to think like a chicken and at the end die like one of them. He was not born to be controlled by the farmer. The little boy was not the eagle egg that a farmer stole from its nest and placed in a prairie chicken nest.

Through all the difficulties that he endured he found the golden secret at the end. This is the secret that each one of you must find by your own effort. Because that secret cannot be told.

That little boy of the story is me. I am a young man, thirty-four years old, with higher education, lots of valuable experiences and wisdom.

Today instead of one house, I have eleven properties around the world; instead of one old bicycle, I have luxury cars and money. Today I own a successful company, I have become a businessman, I am a poet and a professional athlete.

Every day I am freer than the day before, with a soul full of joy and love.

I have learned the secret and now will only walk in that path. With every step further that I go, my life is getting better.

Today I have a new desire and that's to teach you how to find the path to ultimate success, and learn to love yourself and your life no matter what situation you are in, and don't judge it, just watch it, be happy and enjoy each moment – and follow the rules in this book.

Truth about me ...

I am irreligious and atheist
I am a mendicant in the street
Love is my food
and pain is my medicine
The entire world is my spirit
and day goes as I wish
I'm the Lord and the king
I am, myself the God
I am the pain and the torment
I am happiness and treasure
I am tired and alone
I am a mountain and a sea
Satan is me
I worship the devil
I am the soul of Ahura
I am a field and a desert
I am a worm
I have a pure and sincere heart
I am a lion and a wolf
I am a tree and a leaf
I am the soul of God and
I am the God
I am the voice of thunder
I am the meaning of prosperity
I am Jehovah
I am the sin
I am demiurge of hell and
I am the lord of inferno
I am the king of heaven
my temperament is from fire
I am the stars
I am the predators
I am the lord of Love
I am the rehearsal
I am all the existence
I am the apogee and the humility
I am the hand of God
and righteousness is my voice
I am the lord of lords

I am the light and the moon
I am the earth
I am filthy and purity
I am the murder and
I am the creator of bread
I am the God
Hear my voice
I, myself am the one
Then don't say where? or Who?
(By: Sia R.)

First of all love yourself, whoever you are because you are unique the way you are. Accept yourself completely without labeling it good or bad. Universe lives in you!

Learn to free yourself from the control of external factors. When you have made sure that your choices are not influenced by people around you, surroundings and circumstances then choose your target. It won't be easy, but it's the first step. When you've chosen your goal, begin. On the way to achieving great success you may be humiliated, you will suffer, you will be accused and there will pain.

Just like a piece of steel that's going to become a sword and it's not a sword at first, the process begins with heating the steel in a forge and then it is hammered into shape and placed into a quenching tank. This quenching allows it to cool quickly and evenly, which will harden the steel. The sword is repeatedly hammered and heated until it comes into the desired shape and this is required by the metal to keep the desired properties of strength and flexibility.

However difficult the situation becomes, you should not give up, just continue and continue. This is the law of our universe and it won't be without pain.

The people around you will cause you pain, your surroundings will give you great affliction, but you are strong and you will go forward.

You are unbeatable; you will achieve whatever you desire. You should know that throughout the history all the great leaders, all the great minds and all the great achievers have faced difficulties and suffered.

So be great, man, be great, because this is the only truth of your being.

Printed in the United States
By Bookmasters